Mr. Gauguin's Heart

MARIE-DANIELLE CROTEAU

Mr. Gauguin's Heart

Illustrated by ISABELLE ARSENAULT

Translated by SUSAN OURIOU

TUNDRA BOOKS

Originally published in French as *Le coeur de monsieur Gauguin* by les éditions Les 400 coups, Montreal, 2004
First published in this edition by Tundra Books, Toronto, 2007

Published in Canada by Tundra Books,
75 Sherbourne Street, Toronto, Ontario M5A 2P9

Published in the United States by Tundra Books of Northern New York,
P.O. Box 1030, Plattsburgh, New York 12901

Library of Congress Control Number: 2006909134

Library and Archives Canada Cataloguing in Publication

Croteau, Marie-Danielle, 1953–
[Coeur de monsieur Gauguin. English]
    Mr. Gauguin's heart / Marie-Danielle Croteau ; illustrated by
Isabelle Arsenault ; translated by Susan Ouriou.

Translation of: Le coeur de monsieur Gauguin.
ISBN 978-0-88776-824-8

    1. Gauguin, Paul, 1848-1903 – Childhood and youth – Juvenile fiction.
I. Arsenault, Isabelle, 1978– II. Ouriou, Susan III. Title.

PS8555.R6185C6313 2007   jC843'.54   C2006-905782-6

We acknowledge the financial support of the Government of Canada through the
Book Publishing Industry Development Program (BPIDP) and that of the Government of
Ontario through the Ontario Media Development Corporation's Ontario Book Initiative.
We further acknowledge the support of the Canada Council for the Arts and the
Ontario Arts Council for our publishing program.

ONTARIO ARTS COUNCIL
CONSEIL DES ARTS DE L'ONTARIO

Printed and bound in China

1 2 3 4 5 6   12 11 10 09 08 07

For Liane, who sure would take great care of the little orange dog
MARIE–DANIELLE

To my father
ISABELLE

For my invisible friends
SUSAN

In the century before this one, in a land called Denmark, there lived a young boy whose name was Paul Gauguin. He had parents he adored, a sister, Marie, whom he loved (although they squabbled constantly), and a dog. A dog that no one but Paul ever saw. An odd-looking, little orange dog that Paul took everywhere. He had conversations with his dog, he patted his dog, and because of his dog, he was never bored.

The day came when the Gauguin family left Denmark for Peru. The boat journey took a long time, but Paul's imaginary friend kept him busy. The little orange dog hid under passengers' chairs and nibbled on their shoes, or it nipped into galleys making off with strings of sausages. Whenever his little dog behaved badly, Paul would take it back to his cabin. There, he'd play with his spinning tops, leaf through a book, or draw a few pictures. Eventually, the little boy would feel the urge to be up and about again. Pretending to walk his dog, he'd go back to the ship's bridge.

The ship's passengers smiled to see Paul so attached to a dog that didn't exist. They never thought he was peculiar. To them, he just had a vivid imagination. At times, they pretended that they, too, could see the little orange dog, and they'd offer it biscuits that would lie untouched on the carpeted floor.

One afternoon during the crossing, Paul found his mother in tears. She told Paul and his sister that their daddy had been carried away.

"How?" the children cried.

"It was his heart," Mrs. Gauguin answered.

Marie threw herself, wailing, into her mother's arms. Paul said nothing. He didn't understand what it all meant. He didn't see how being carried away by one's heart could be such a tragedy. He took refuge on the ship's bridge with his dog and stared at the horizon. Suddenly, he saw a huge red balloon floating in the distance. Holding on to the balloon was his father.

At the same time, the passengers exclaimed, "Look at that beautiful sun!"

But to Paul, the sun they were pointing to was his father's heart.

Paul ran to find his mother. He couldn't wait to comfort her with the news that his father wasn't lost at all, but was sailing through the sky. He, himself, had seen his father carried away on the wind by his big heart.

Mrs. Gauguin hugged her son close to her. She didn't know how to explain death to him, so instead she said nothing. She took her little boy's outstretched hand, and she and Marie followed him outside. Paul led them to the ship's stem at the very front of the ship, a place he'd discovered one day as he was chasing his dog. It was his favorite spot of all because the whole sea lay ahead of him, waiting to be crossed. The sea behind him, on the other hand, had already become part of his past. When the giant sun slid into the ocean, Paul said, "I'll see you again tomorrow."

Mrs. Gauguin, unsure whether Paul was saying good-bye to the sun or to his father's heart, started to cry all over again.

The next day and the next day after that and, still, the next day after that, Mrs. Gauguin and Marie cried endlessly. But not Paul. He was waiting for his daddy. He spent his days at the ship's stem with his little orange dog, awaiting the sun. People felt sorry for him. Although some asked him about his dog, no one brought him any more biscuits. To them, the time for make-believe had passed.

When they finally reached their destination in Peru, Paul refused to leave the ship. Until, that is, an old man came and took him by the hand. He told the boy to call for his dog. "Your dog needs to get out and run!" he said. "Just like you do!"

He led Paul onto the dock while Marie and Mrs. Gauguin followed at a distance.

Paul wanted to cry out that it wasn't true! He didn't have a dog and had never had one. But the nice old man seemed to believe in his dog so strongly, Paul didn't want to disappoint him.

At the entrance to a great big park, the old man stopped and said, "I'll be waiting for you here at eight o'clock tomorrow morning. Don't be late! And don't forget your dog!"

Paul turned to his mother as she approached them. She nodded and waved good-bye to the old man, then she, Paul, and Marie continued on their way.

The next day, she took Paul to the meeting place. Before leaving, she handed him a basket and planted a kiss on his cheek. Then she went back to their new home, where Marie was waiting for her.

The old man was already stationed by the pond. He had set up an easel and was working on a painting. Paul drew near without making a sound. He didn't want to disturb the old man, so he sat down on a bench and watched.

The old man seemed oblivious to him. He kept right on working, all the while ignoring Paul. Just when Paul was starting to fidget, without turning around, the old man said, "Your turn now. Draw me a picture of your dog."

"But I don't have anything to paint with," Paul protested. "Not any paint or brushes or a smock. Not a thing!"

"Look in your basket," the old man said.

A surprised Paul did as he was told. Instead of just the snack he expected to see, inside the basket was everything he needed to paint and draw. The little boy offered an orange to his new companion.

"What about that!" said the old man. "It's the same color as your dog."

He mixed red and yellow together on his palette. "Painting is magic," he said to Paul. "You can start with next to nothing and still do anything you want."

The little boy looked the old man straight in the eye. "Even bring something to life?"

"Yes, you can bring things to life," he replied. "Or prolong the life they had."

The old man took a paintbrush and drew a picture of an orange on the white canvas. Then he peeled his own orange and ate it. "You see, my orange is gone and yet it isn't. I still have this one." He stepped aside. "Your turn now. Draw me your dog."

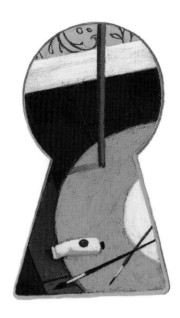

Back home, Paul shut himself in his room.

"What are you up to in there?" his mother asked, a tad worried.

"Making magic!" the little boy answered.

Through the door, she heard her son move objects around.
Then all of a sudden she heard nothing but silence.

After a minute or so, unable to wait any longer, she knocked on
the door.

"Just a second!" yelled Paul. "I'm almost through. . . ."

A few short minutes later, he opened the door to let his
mother in.

On a makeshift easel stood a painting of the ocean. Above
the ocean was a large red circle that was the spitting image of
a setting sun.

Mrs. Gauguin's face lit up. Seeing his mother's smile, Paul realized that he wanted to be a magician.

Many people came to visit the Gauguin family in Peru. And all who came admired the little boy's painting. Since they knew nothing about affairs of the heart, they assumed he had painted a picture of Japan's national flag.

Years later, Paul would become one of the greatest painters of his time. It is said that his art resembles that of Japan. But what no one knows — other than you and Mrs. Gauguin — is that the red sun he painted all those years ago does not represent the flag of a faraway nation. The little boy's painting of the big red sun is really a picture of Mr. Gauguin's heart.